TECH DEMYSTIFIED

A Layman's Guide to Navigating Smartphones and Computers

Unlock the Power of Modern Technology with Confidence and Ease

Nathan R. Jankins

CONTENTS

INTRODUCTION   6

I. EMBRACING TECHNOLOGY   9

   Understanding the Benefits of Technology in Everyday Life   9

   Overcoming Technophobia and Building Confidence   13

II. DEMYSTIFYING SMARTPHONES   17

   Smartphone Basics: Buttons, Touchscreens and Interfaces   17

   Navigating Through Different Smartphone Models and Brands   21

   Customizing Settings and Personalization   25

III. MASTERING THE BASICS   29

   Making and Receiving Calls   29

   Sending and Receiving Messages (SMS, MMS, Instant Messaging)   33

   Setting Up Voicemail   37

IV. ESSENTIAL APPS AND FEATURES   41

   Exploring the Most Useful Pre-installed Apps   41

   Installing and Managing New Apps   46

   Understanding App Permissions and Privacy   50

V. INTERNET AND ONLINE SAFETY   54

   Connecting to Wi-Fi and Mobile Data   54

Browsing the Internet: URLs, Search Engines, and Bookmarks 59

Staying Safe Online: Avoiding Scams and Phishing 63

VI. SOCIAL MEDIA 101   68

Introduction to Popular Social Media Platforms 68

Creating and Managing Social Media Accounts 72

Understanding Privacy Settings and Sharing Responsibly 77

VII. MASTERING MESSAGING APPS   82

Using WhatsApp, Messenger and Other Messaging Platforms 82

Sending Photos, Videos and Voice Messages 88

Making Voice and Video Calls Through Messaging Apps 92

VIII. COMPUTERS MADE EASY   97

Introduction to Desktops, Laptops and Operating Systems 97

Navigating the Desktop: Icons, Taskbar and Start Menu 101

Using Files and Folders: Creating, Organizing and Searching 105

IX. INTERNET AND EMAIL BASICS   109

Accessing the Internet and Browsing with Browsers 109

Setting Up and Using Email Accounts 114

Sending, Receiving and Managing Emails 118

X. TROUBLESHOOTING TIPS   122

Common Smartphone and Computer Issues and How to Fix Them 122

When and Where to Seek Technical Support 126

    Maintaining the Performance and Security of Devices   *130*

XI. STAYING SAFE AND SECURE   **135**

    Protecting Devices with Passwords and Biometrics   *135*

    Understanding Antivirus and Security Software   *139*

    Best Practices for Safeguarding Personal Information   *143*

XII. BEYOND BASICS: FUN AND PRODUCTIVITY   **148**

    Exploring Advanced Features and Tools   *148*

    Using Smartphones and Computers for Productivity Tasks   *152*

    Entertainment Options: Streaming Media and Gaming   *157*

CONCLUSION   **161**

INTRODUCTION

In this fast-paced digital age, technology surrounds us, shaping the way we connect, work, and navigate the world. Smartphones and computers have become our loyal companions, opening up new horizons of possibilities and enhancing our daily lives. Yet, for many of us, the world of technology can seem like an intimidating maze, filled with confusing jargon and complex functions.

If you've ever felt overwhelmed by the ever-evolving tech landscape, fear not! "Tech Demystified: A Layman's Guide to Navigating Smartphones and Computers" is here to be your trusted navigator, leading you through the captivating world of modern technology with confidence and ease.

Whether you're a tech novice or someone seeking to refine their digital skills, this guide is tailored to meet you at your level. Our mission is simple: to break down the barriers between you and technology, empowering you to harness its full potential without frustration.

What You'll Find Inside:

We've designed this guide to be your comprehensive resource for understanding and utilizing smartphones and computers effectively. You'll embark on a journey of discovery, exploring the fundamentals of these devices, the most essential features, and practical applications to enrich your personal and professional life.

Step-by-step, we'll take you through the basics, so you can confidently make calls, send messages, access the internet, and explore social media. You'll master the art of personalization, customizing your devices to suit your preferences and lifestyle.

But we won't stop at the basics. We'll delve into the world of apps, unveiling a treasure trove of useful tools and entertainment at your fingertips. Whether you're looking to manage finances, enhance productivity, or indulge in hobbies, we'll guide you through app selection and use.

Your safety and security are paramount. We'll equip you with practical tips to navigate the online realm with confidence, safeguarding your personal information and privacy.

And when you encounter roadblocks along the way, fear not! Troubleshooting tips and support will be at your disposal to overcome any technical challenges.

Embrace Technology with Confidence:

The true power of technology lies in its ability to enrich our lives and make the complex seem simple. We believe that anyone can embrace technology with confidence and joy. With this guide as your companion, you'll transform from a hesitant user into a savvy navigator, exploring the vast digital landscape with a newfound sense of empowerment.

So, let's embark on this exciting journey together. Unravel the mysteries of technology, and unlock its full potential. "Tech Demystified: A Layman's Guide to Navigating Smartphones and Computers" is here to show you the way.

Welcome aboard!

I. EMBRACING TECHNOLOGY

Understanding the Benefits of Technology in Everyday Life

In the fast-paced and interconnected world we live in, technology has become an indispensable part of our daily routines. It has revolutionized how we communicate, work, learn, and entertain ourselves. In this section, we'll delve deeper into the numerous advantages that technology offers in our everyday lives:

1. **Communication and Connectivity**: Technology has transformed the way we connect with one another. With smartphones, social media, video conferencing, and messaging apps, we can instantly reach out to friends, family, and colleagues, regardless of geographical boundaries. Communication is now seamless, enabling us to stay connected with our loved ones and build global networks.

2. **Information Access**: The internet has made vast amounts of information accessible at our fingertips. From academic

research to DIY tutorials, we can learn about virtually anything with a simple online search. This wealth of knowledge empowers us to make informed decisions and broaden our understanding of the world.

3. **Convenience and Efficiency**: Technology has streamlined our daily tasks, making them more efficient and time-saving. From online banking and shopping to ride-hailing apps and home automation, technology has simplified various aspects of our lives, freeing up time for more meaningful pursuits.

4. **Health and Well-being**: Advancements in medical technology have improved healthcare outcomes and enhanced our well-being. Wearable health devices, telemedicine, and health tracking apps help us monitor and manage our health, empowering us to lead healthier lifestyles.

5. **Productivity and Work Flexibility**: Technology has revolutionized the way we work, allowing for remote work and flexible schedules. Collaboration tools, cloud computing, and project management software enable teams

to work seamlessly regardless of their physical locations, boosting productivity and work-life balance.

6. **Education and E-Learning**: Online learning platforms and educational apps have made education more accessible to people worldwide. With the ability to take courses from renowned institutions without geographical constraints, lifelong learning has become a reality.

7. **Entertainment and Creativity**: Technology has opened up a vast array of entertainment options. From streaming services and gaming to digital art and content creation, technology fuels creativity and provides entertainment tailored to individual preferences.

8. **Environmental Impact**: Technology has the potential to address environmental challenges. Sustainable practices, renewable energy solutions, and smart devices contribute to reducing our carbon footprint and fostering a greener future.

9. **Social and Cultural Impact**: Technology has brought diverse cultures closer together, allowing for cross-cultural exchange and fostering understanding and empathy among people worldwide. Social media platforms enable us to

engage with a global audience and share our unique perspectives.

10. **Innovation and Progress**: Technological advancements continually push the boundaries of human potential. Innovations in artificial intelligence, robotics, and biotechnology hold the promise of shaping a brighter and more sustainable future.

Understanding and appreciating these benefits can help us embrace technology with enthusiasm and optimism. As we navigate our digital lives, recognizing the positive impact of technology empowers us to harness its potential responsibly and use it as a force for good in both our personal and collective journeys. Technology is a tool, and how we wield it determines the outcomes it brings into our lives. With this awareness, we embark on a journey of exploration and growth, eager to make the most of the boundless opportunities technology presents.

Overcoming Technophobia and Building Confidence

Technophobia, the fear or aversion to technology, is a common hurdle that many people face when navigating the digital landscape. This fear can stem from various factors, such as unfamiliarity with devices, concerns about privacy and security, or apprehension about making mistakes. However, with the right approach and guidance, technophobia can be conquered, paving the way for newfound confidence and empowerment in using technology. In this section, we'll explore key strategies to overcome technophobia and build the confidence needed to embrace technology with ease:

1. **Education and Familiarization**: One of the most effective ways to combat technophobia is through education and familiarization. Taking the time to learn about the basics of technology, how devices work, and their essential functions can demystify the technology landscape. Guided tutorials, online courses, or workshops tailored for beginners can be valuable resources to gain a foundational understanding.

2. **Positive Mindset and Patience**: Embracing technology requires a positive mindset and patience with oneself. It's essential to remember that everyone starts as a beginner,

and making mistakes is a natural part of the learning process. Instead of viewing challenges as failures, consider them as opportunities for growth and improvement.

3. **Start Small and Gradual Progression**: Beginning with simple tasks and gradually progressing to more complex ones can help ease technophobia. Start by performing basic functions on smartphones or computers, such as making calls, sending texts, or navigating the internet. Gradually introduce new features and apps as you become more comfortable.

4. **Seek Support and Guidance**: Don't hesitate to seek support and guidance from friends, family, or tech-savvy individuals. Engaging in conversations about technology and asking for help when needed can boost your confidence and create a supportive learning environment.

5. **Explore Your Interests**: Tailor your technology exploration to align with your interests and passions. Whether it's using technology for hobbies, learning about topics of personal interest, or connecting with like-minded communities online, focusing on what excites you can make the learning process more enjoyable.

6. **Practice Regularly**: Like any skill, proficiency in using technology comes with practice. Set aside regular time to interact with your devices and explore various features. The more you use technology in your daily life, the more confident and adept you'll become.

7. **Recognize the Benefits**: Remind yourself of the benefits that technology offers in enhancing your life. Embracing technology can improve communication, increase productivity, and provide endless learning opportunities. Understanding how technology enriches your life can serve as motivation to overcome technophobia.

8. **Celebrate Your Progress**: Celebrate your achievements and progress, no matter how small they may seem. Each step you take toward embracing technology represents a milestone in your journey. Acknowledge your efforts and growth as you become a more confident navigator in the digital world.

By implementing these strategies, you'll gradually build confidence and overcome technophobia. Remember that technology is a tool designed to make our lives easier and more fulfilling. Embracing it with confidence allows you to harness its full potential, opening doors to countless opportunities and enriching experiences.

II. DEMYSTIFYING SMARTPHONES

Smartphone Basics: Buttons, Touchscreens and Interfaces

Smartphones have evolved into incredibly versatile and user-friendly devices, but for newcomers, the array of buttons, touch gestures, and interfaces may appear overwhelming. In this section, we'll guide you through the fundamental elements of smartphones, making them more approachable and accessible:

1. Physical Buttons:

- **Power Button**: Located typically on the side or top of the phone, the power button is used to turn the device on or off. A long press of this button may also bring up options to restart the phone or switch it to airplane mode.

- **Volume Controls**: Most smartphones have dedicated volume buttons to adjust the sound level for ringtones, notifications, and media. These buttons can also be used to take photos when the camera app is active.

- **Home Button**: While some modern smartphones do not have a physical home button, older models might still feature one at the bottom of the screen. Pressing the home button typically takes you to the home screen, where you can access apps and features.

2. Touchscreen Gestures:

- **Tapping**: A single tap on the touchscreen selects or opens an app or item.

- **Swiping**: Moving your finger across the screen in various directions can be used to scroll through content, navigate menus, or switch between screens.

- **Pinching**: Placing two fingers close together on the screen and then spreading them apart is called pinching. This gesture is often used to zoom in or out on photos or webpages.

- **Multi-Finger Gestures**: Some smartphones support multi-finger gestures like swiping with three fingers to take a screenshot or using multiple fingers to control certain features.

3. User Interface (UI):

- **Home Screen**: When you unlock your smartphone, the first thing you see is the home screen. This is the central hub from which you access apps, widgets, and shortcuts.

- **App Icons**: App icons are visual representations of the apps installed on your smartphone. Tapping an icon opens the corresponding app.

- **Notification Center**: Swipe down from the top of the screen to access the notification center, which displays incoming notifications from apps like messages, emails, and social media updates.

- **Quick Settings Panel**: Also accessed by swiping down from the top of the screen, the quick settings panel allows you to toggle various settings like Wi-Fi, Bluetooth, airplane mode, and more.

Understanding these basic smartphone elements is essential for effective navigation and interaction with your device. As you become more familiar with the physical buttons and touch gestures, you'll gain confidence in using your smartphone seamlessly. Moreover, comprehending the user interface will allow you to customize your home screen, manage notifications, and access essential features effortlessly.

Navigating Through Different Smartphone Models and Brands

With an abundance of smartphone models and brands available in the market, choosing the right one that aligns with your needs and preferences can be a daunting task. In this section, we'll guide you through the process of exploring various smartphone options, understanding key features, and making an informed decision:

1. Comparing Features and Specifications:

- **Display Size and Resolution**: Consider the display size and resolution that suits your preferences. Larger screens offer more immersive media experiences, while smaller screens are more pocket-friendly.

- **Camera Quality**: If photography is a priority for you, pay attention to the camera specifications. Look for features like megapixels, aperture size, image stabilization, and camera modes.

- **Battery Life**: Long-lasting battery life ensures that your smartphone can keep up with your busy schedule without constantly needing to recharge.

- **Performance and Processing Power**: The processor and RAM play a crucial role in the smartphone's performance and multitasking capabilities. A powerful processor and sufficient RAM ensure smooth performance.

- **Storage Capacity**: Evaluate the storage options available and choose a smartphone with adequate internal storage or one that allows for expandable storage with a microSD card.

2. Operating Systems:

- **iOS (Apple)**: iPhones run on Apple's iOS, known for its user-friendly interface, seamless integration with other Apple devices, and a curated app ecosystem. iOS devices receive regular software updates for security and new features.

- **Android (Google)**: Android smartphones offer a wide variety of brands and models with varying features and price ranges. Android's customizable interface, extensive app selection on the Google Play Store, and compatibility with various devices make it a popular choice.

- **Others (Windows, etc.)**: While iOS and Android dominate the smartphone market, there are alternative operating systems like Windows or KaiOS. These may be present in select devices, offering unique features or catering to specific user preferences.

3. Brand Considerations:

- **Reliability and Reputation**: Consider reputable brands known for reliable build quality, software updates, and customer support. Established brands often have a track record of producing reliable and high-quality smartphones.

- **Customer Reviews**: Look for user reviews and ratings of specific smartphone models to gain insights into real-world experiences and satisfaction levels.

- **Brand Ecosystem**: Some users prefer a brand that offers a broader ecosystem of devices and services, allowing for seamless integration and data synchronization across devices.

4. Budget Considerations:

- **Price Range**: Determine your budget and explore smartphone models within that range. Smartphones are available at various price points, from budget-friendly options to high-end flagship devices.

- **Previous Generation Models**: Consider purchasing a previous-generation model, which may offer excellent features at a more affordable price after a newer model is released.

Exploring different smartphone models and brands can be an exciting journey. Take your time to research and compare features to find a smartphone that suits your needs and aligns with your budget. Keep in mind that there is no one-size-fits-all solution, and the best smartphone for you is the one that meets your specific requirements and preferences.

Customizing Settings and Personalization

Your smartphone is more than just a device; it's an extension of your personality and preferences. In this section, we'll explore the exciting world of customizing settings and personalizing your smartphone to make it uniquely yours:

1. Setting Up Your Device:

- **Initial Setup**: When you first turn on your new smartphone, you'll be guided through the initial setup process. This includes selecting your language, connecting to Wi-Fi or mobile data, and signing in or creating an account with your preferred email or social media account.

- **Security and Privacy**: Set up security features like a PIN, password, pattern, or fingerprint unlock to protect your smartphone from unauthorized access. You can also configure privacy settings to control how apps access your data and permissions.

2. Personalizing Your Home Screen:

- **Wallpapers**: Choose a wallpaper that resonates with your style and preferences. You can select from a variety of pre-installed wallpapers or use your favorite photos as the background.

- **Widgets**: Widgets are handy tools that provide at-a-glance information or quick access to app features. Customize your home screen by adding widgets for weather, calendar events, news, and more.

- **App Icons**: Organize and personalize your app icons by rearranging them or grouping them into folders. You can even change the appearance of app icons using icon packs from the app store.

3. Themes and Visual Customization:

- **Themes**: Many smartphones allow you to apply pre-designed themes that change the overall look and feel of your device. Themes can alter the wallpaper, icon styles, and system colors to create a cohesive and visually pleasing interface.

- **Live Wallpapers**: Live wallpapers add movement and interactivity to your home screen, making it more dynamic and engaging. Choose from animated nature scenes, interactive patterns, or 3D effects.

4. App Management and Organization:

- **Uninstalling Apps**: Remove unnecessary apps from your smartphone to declutter your home screen and free up storage space. Apps that come pre-installed and cannot be uninstalled can often be disabled to reduce clutter.

- **Creating Folders**: Organize your apps by creating folders based on categories or usage. For example, you can have a folder for social media apps, another for productivity tools, and so on.

5. Notifications and Do Not Disturb:

- **Notification Settings**: Tailor your notification preferences by choosing which apps can send you alerts and adjusting the type of notifications you receive. This ensures that you stay informed without feeling overwhelmed.

- **Do Not Disturb**: Use the Do Not Disturb feature to set specific hours during which you won't receive notifications or calls. This feature is useful when you want uninterrupted time for work, sleep, or relaxation.

By customizing settings and personalizing your smartphone, you'll create a user experience that aligns with your lifestyle and aesthetics. Your smartphone will become an extension of your identity, reflecting your unique style and preferences. As you explore the various customization options, you'll discover new ways to make your digital experience more enjoyable and tailored to your needs.

III. MASTERING THE BASICS

Making and Receiving Calls

Making and receiving calls is one of the most fundamental and essential functions of a smartphone. It allows you to connect with friends, family, colleagues, and business contacts easily. Let's explore the details of making and receiving calls on your smartphone:

1. Dialing a Number:

- To make a call, open the Phone app on your smartphone. It is usually represented by an icon with a green phone receiver.
- Use the on-screen keypad to enter the phone number you wish to call. You can type the number directly or select it from your contacts by tapping on the contact's name.
- After entering the number, tap the call button, which is typically represented by a green phone icon. This will initiate the call, and the recipient's phone will start ringing.

2. Answering Calls:

- When you receive an incoming call, your smartphone's screen will display the caller's information. This includes the caller's phone number or contact name if it is saved in your address book.
- To answer the call, you have several options:
    - Swipe the green phone icon to the right to accept the call. This gesture is commonly known as "swipe to answer."
    - If your smartphone has physical buttons, you can press the designated answer call button (usually located on the side or front of the device).
    - Some smartphones may also have an on-screen button with the label "Answer" or a phone icon that you can tap to answer the call.

3. Ending Calls:

- To end a call, you can use one of the following methods:
    - Tap the red phone icon on the screen to hang up the call.

- If your smartphone has physical buttons, press the designated end call button to disconnect the call.
- On some devices, you may be able to use a gesture like "swipe to end call" by swiping the red phone icon to the right.

4. Call Features:

- During a call, your smartphone offers various call features to enhance your experience:
    - **Hold**: If you need to momentarily put the call on hold, you can tap the "Hold" button or icon. This feature is useful when you need to attend to another matter without ending the call.
    - **Mute**: The mute button allows you to mute your microphone so that the other party cannot hear you. This feature is handy when you need to discuss something privately or when you are in a noisy environment.
    - **Speakerphone**: By tapping the speakerphone icon, you can switch to the speaker mode, allowing you

to have hands-free conversations without holding the phone to your ear.

Mastering the art of making and receiving calls on your smartphone is a foundational skill that opens the door to seamless communication with others. Whether it's for personal or professional use, being comfortable with making and receiving calls ensures that you can stay connected with your contacts whenever you need to. As you continue to explore the world of technology, you'll find that smartphones offer a wide range of features and possibilities to enhance your communication experience.

Sending and Receiving Messages (SMS, MMS, Instant Messaging)

Messaging on smartphones provides a versatile and convenient way to communicate with others. Let's explore the various types of messaging options available and how to use them effectively:

1. SMS (Short Message Service):

- SMS, commonly known as text messaging, allows you to send and receive text-only messages to and from other mobile phone users.
- To send an SMS, open the messaging app on your smartphone, compose a new message, enter the recipient's phone number or select their contact name from your address book, type your message, and then tap the send button.
- SMS messages are typically limited to 160 characters per message, but modern smartphones automatically split longer messages into multiple parts for seamless delivery.

2. MMS (Multimedia Messaging Service):

- MMS enables you to send multimedia content, such as photos, videos, audio files, and contact cards, along with your text message.
- To send an MMS, follow similar steps as sending an SMS, but attach the multimedia content before tapping the send button.
- Keep in mind that MMS messages may have additional charges if your mobile plan does not include unlimited MMS.

3. Instant Messaging Apps:

- Instant messaging apps offer a more feature-rich and interactive way to communicate with others over the internet.
- Popular instant messaging apps include WhatsApp, Facebook Messenger, Telegram, Signal, and many others. These apps allow you to send text messages, multimedia files, voice messages, and even make voice or video calls using an internet connection (Wi-Fi or mobile data).

- To use instant messaging apps, you'll need to download and install the app from your smartphone's app store. After installing the app, create an account, and then you can start messaging your contacts who are also using the same app.

4. Group Messaging:

- Most messaging apps, including SMS, MMS, and instant messaging apps, support group messaging. You can create group chats with multiple contacts, making it easy to communicate with friends, family, or colleagues simultaneously.

5. Message Settings:

- You can customize your message settings to enhance your messaging experience:
    - **Notifications**: Adjust notification settings to receive alerts for new messages in your preferred way, such as sound, vibration, or pop-up notifications.

- **Delivery Reports**: Enable delivery reports to receive confirmation when your messages are successfully delivered to the recipient's device.
- **Read Receipts**: Some messaging apps offer read receipts, which notify you when the recipient has read your message.
- **Auto-Download**: Manage auto-download settings for multimedia content to control when photos and videos are automatically downloaded.

By exploring the various messaging options available, you can choose the method that best suits your needs and preferences. Whether you prefer the simplicity of SMS or the rich features of instant messaging apps, messaging on your smartphone offers a convenient and efficient way to stay connected with friends, family, and colleagues.

Setting Up Voicemail

Setting up voicemail is essential to ensure that callers can leave you voice messages when you are unavailable or unable to answer your phone. Voicemail setup may vary slightly depending on your mobile carrier and smartphone model, but the general process is as follows:

1. Contact Your Carrier:

- To set up voicemail, you'll need to contact your mobile carrier or service provider. Dial the customer service number provided by your carrier or visit their website for instructions on setting up voicemail.

2. Access Voicemail Setup:

- Once you've reached your carrier's customer service, follow the prompts to set up your voicemail. You may be asked to enter your phone number, account information, or a security PIN for verification.

3. Record a Personalized Greeting:

- After verification, you'll be prompted to record a personalized voicemail greeting. This is the message that callers will hear when they reach your voicemail. You can use the default greeting or record your custom message.

4. Set Up Voicemail PIN (Optional):

- Some carriers may ask you to set up a personal identification number (PIN) for added security. The PIN ensures that only you can access your voicemail messages. Choose a PIN that you can remember but is not easily guessable by others.

5. Accessing Voicemail:

- To access your voicemail, dial your own phone number or a specific voicemail access number provided by your carrier. You may also find a voicemail icon or shortcut in your phone's dialer or messaging app that allows you to access voicemail directly.

6. Managing Voicemail Messages:

- When you access your voicemail, you'll hear your personalized greeting followed by any new voicemail messages. Listen to the voicemail messages, and follow the prompts to manage them.
- You can typically save important messages, delete unwanted messages, or call back the person who left the message directly from the voicemail menu.

7. Visual Voicemail (Optional):

- Some smartphones and carriers offer visual voicemail, which displays voicemail messages as a list you can interact with directly on your screen.
- With visual voicemail, you can play, pause, and delete messages directly from the voicemail list without dialing into your voicemail box.

8. Voicemail Notification:

- Your smartphone will often provide a visual or audible notification when you have a new voicemail message. This ensures that you are aware of missed calls and can promptly check your voicemail.

Following these steps will help you set up your voicemail and ensure that you don't miss important messages when you're unable to answer your phone. It's a valuable feature that enhances your communication capabilities and ensures that callers can reach you even when you're unavailable. As you continue to explore the features of your smartphone, you'll find that it offers various tools to stay connected and organized.

IV. ESSENTIAL APPS AND FEATURES

Exploring the Most Useful Pre-installed Apps

Your smartphone comes with a variety of pre-installed apps that are designed to be useful right out of the box. These apps cater to essential functionalities and are ready to be used as soon as you set up your device. Let's explore some of the most useful pre-installed apps on smartphones:

1. Phone:

- The Phone app is the gateway to making and receiving calls. It allows you to dial phone numbers, access your call log, and manage various call features such as call waiting and call forwarding.

2. Contacts:

- The Contacts app is your digital address book. It stores and organizes the contact information of your friends, family, colleagues, and other important contacts. You can add, edit, and manage contact details, making it easy to call or message them with just a few taps.

3. Messaging:

- The Messaging app enables you to send and receive text messages (SMS) and multimedia messages (MMS). It's a basic yet essential tool for staying connected through text-based communication.

4. Camera:

- The Camera app allows you to capture photos and record videos using your smartphone's built-in camera. Depending on the smartphone model, it may offer various shooting modes, filters, and editing features to enhance your photography experience.

5. Gallery (or Photos):

- The Gallery app lets you view, organize, and manage your photos and videos. You can create albums, delete unwanted media, and share your favorite moments with friends and family.

6. Email:

- The Email app provides access to your email accounts, allowing you to send, receive, and manage emails on your smartphone. You can sync multiple email accounts, and some apps even support email threading for better organization.

7. Calendar:

- The Calendar app helps you manage your schedule and stay organized. You can schedule events, appointments, and reminders, making it easier to keep track of your daily activities.

8. Clock:

- The Clock app serves as an alarm clock, timer, stopwatch, and world clock. It's a versatile tool for managing time-related tasks and ensuring you wake up on time or stay punctual for appointments.

9. Maps:

- The Maps app offers navigation, directions, and location services. You can find places, get driving directions, explore nearby points of interest, and even use the app offline in some cases.

10. Internet Browser:

- The Internet browser is your window to the web. It allows you to search for information, visit websites, and access online services on your smartphone.

These pre-installed apps provide a strong foundation for your smartphone's functionalities and productivity. As you become familiar with these apps, you'll find that they meet most of your everyday needs. However, there are countless other apps available in the app stores that cater to specific interests and hobbies, offering even more functionality and customization for your smartphone experience.

Installing and Managing New Apps

Installing new apps on your smartphone allows you to customize and expand its functionalities to suit your specific needs and interests. Managing these apps ensures that your device remains organized and optimized for performance. Here's a step-by-step guide on how to install and manage new apps on your smartphone:

1. Accessing the App Store:

- On Android devices, open the Google Play Store. On iOS devices (iPhone and iPad), open the Apple App Store. You can usually find the app store icon on your home screen or in the app drawer.

2. Browsing and Searching for Apps:

- Use the search bar to look for specific apps or explore the featured, top charts, or categories sections to discover new apps.
- Read app descriptions, reviews, and ratings to ensure you download trusted and reliable apps.

3. Downloading and Installing Apps:

- Once you've found the app you want, tap on it to view more details. If the app is free, you'll see a "Install" or "Get" button. For paid apps, the button will display the app's price.
- Tap the appropriate button to initiate the download and installation process.
- Your smartphone may ask for your fingerprint, passcode, or face recognition (on devices equipped with Face ID) to verify the download.

4. App Permissions:

- During the installation process, you may be prompted to grant the app certain permissions to access features or data on your device. Review the permissions carefully, and decide whether the app needs these permissions to function properly.
- For example, a camera app may require access to your device's camera, while a navigation app may need access to your location.

5. Organizing Apps:

- Once you have several apps installed, you can organize them on your home screen or in folders.
- On most smartphones, you can press and hold an app icon to enter "edit" or "arrange" mode, allowing you to move, delete, or place apps in folders.
- Create folders to group similar apps together, such as social media apps, productivity tools, or games.

6. Uninstalling Apps:

- To remove an app from your smartphone, press and hold the app icon, and an option to "uninstall" or "remove" should appear. Tap on it to confirm the uninstallation.
- Alternatively, you can go to your smartphone's settings, find the "Apps" or "Applications" section, select the app you want to remove, and choose "uninstall" from there.

7. App Updates:

- Regularly check for app updates in the app store. App updates often include bug fixes, improvements, and new features.
- You can set your smartphone to automatically update apps or choose to update them manually.

By installing and managing apps on your smartphone, you can tailor your device to suit your preferences and lifestyle. With a vast array of apps available in the app stores, you can explore endless possibilities to enhance your smartphone experience.

Understanding App Permissions and Privacy

Understanding app permissions and privacy is crucial to protect your personal data and ensure the security of your smartphone. When you install a new app, it may request access to certain features or information on your device. Here's what you need to know about app permissions and how to manage them:

1. What Are App Permissions?

- App permissions are the privileges that apps request to access specific features, data, or hardware on your smartphone.
- Common app permissions include access to your camera, microphone, contacts, location, photos, and device sensors.

2. Why Do Apps Need Permissions?

- App permissions are necessary for apps to function properly and provide their intended services.
- For example, a camera app requires access to your device's camera to take photos, and a navigation app needs access to your location to provide accurate directions.

3. Granting Permissions:

- When you install a new app, you'll usually be prompted to grant specific permissions before the app can access certain features or data.
- Review the permission requests carefully and consider whether the app genuinely needs access to the requested features for its core functionality.

4. Managing App Permissions:

- You can manage app permissions on your smartphone to control what data and features apps can access.
- On Android devices, go to Settings > Apps & notifications > [App name] > Permissions to view and adjust app permissions.
- On iOS devices, go to Settings > [App name] > Privacy to manage app permissions.

5. Best Practices for App Permissions:

- Be cautious with sensitive permissions: Some apps may request access to sensitive data, like your contacts or location. Only grant these permissions to apps that you trust and genuinely need them.
- Regularly review app permissions: Periodically check the permissions granted to installed apps and revoke any permissions that are no longer necessary.
- Update your apps: Keep your apps up to date as developers often release updates to improve security and fix vulnerabilities.
- Download from reputable sources: Install apps from official app stores like Google Play Store or Apple App Store, as they have security measures to detect and remove malicious apps.

6. App Privacy Policies:

- Many apps have privacy policies that explain how they collect, use, and share your data. Review the privacy policy before installing an app to understand how your information will be handled.

7. App Permissions and Operating Systems:

- Different versions of operating systems may handle app permissions differently. Make sure your smartphone's operating system is up to date to benefit from the latest privacy features and enhancements.

By being aware of app permissions and managing them effectively, you can protect your personal data and maintain your smartphone's privacy. It's essential to strike a balance between granting necessary permissions for app functionality and safeguarding your sensitive information.

V. INTERNET AND ONLINE SAFETY

Connecting to Wi-Fi and Mobile Data

Connecting to Wi-Fi and mobile data are essential for accessing the internet on your smartphone. Each method has its advantages and use cases.

Connecting to Wi-Fi:

1. Advantages:

- **Faster Speeds**: Wi-Fi connections generally offer faster internet speeds compared to mobile data connections. This is especially beneficial when downloading large files, streaming videos, or using data-intensive apps.
- **Cost Savings**: Connecting to Wi-Fi helps you conserve your mobile data usage, which can be especially useful if you have limited data on your cellular plan.

- **Stable Connection**: Wi-Fi networks, especially in your home or office, tend to provide a more stable and consistent internet connection than mobile data.

2. How to Connect:

- To connect to Wi-Fi, go to your smartphone's settings and find the "Wi-Fi" option. Turn on Wi-Fi if it's not already enabled.
- Your smartphone will scan for available Wi-Fi networks. Select the network you want to join and enter the password if it's a secure network.
- Once connected, your device will remember the network, and it will automatically connect whenever you are in range.

3. Recommended Usage:

- Use Wi-Fi when you are at home, at work, or in locations with public Wi-Fi hotspots. Wi-Fi is ideal for activities that require high-speed internet access, such as streaming, online gaming, and downloading large files.

Connecting to Mobile Data:

1. Advantages:

- **Portability**: Mobile data allows you to access the internet on the go, even when Wi-Fi is unavailable. As long as you have a cellular signal, you can use mobile data anywhere.
- **Convenience**: Mobile data eliminates the need to connect to a specific Wi-Fi network. It is suitable for tasks that require internet access when you are away from home or office.

2. How to Connect:

- To use mobile data, go to your smartphone's settings and find the "Mobile data" or "Cellular data" option. Turn it on if it's not already enabled.

- Your smartphone will connect to your carrier's data network, and you'll be able to access the internet using your cellular plan.

3. Recommended Usage:

- Use mobile data when you are outside, traveling, or in places where Wi-Fi is not available or the Wi-Fi signal is weak. It's also handy for quick internet access for tasks like checking emails, social media, or maps.

Switching Between Wi-Fi and Mobile Data:

Your smartphone can automatically switch between Wi-Fi and mobile data connections based on your location and signal strength. When you are connected to Wi-Fi, your device will prefer using Wi-Fi for data to save mobile data usage. When Wi-Fi is unavailable or weak, your phone will switch to mobile data.

In some cases, you may manually switch between Wi-Fi and mobile data to control your data usage or optimize connection speed. You can do this by turning off Wi-Fi when you want to use mobile data or vice versa.

Data Usage Monitoring:

To avoid exceeding your data plan's limits, monitor your data usage regularly. Smartphones have built-in data usage tracking features that allow you to view your data consumption over a specific period. You can set data usage limits or receive alerts when approaching your data cap.

By understanding how to connect to Wi-Fi and mobile data, you can make the most of your smartphone's internet capabilities and choose the best connectivity option for different scenarios.

Browsing the Internet: URLs, Search Engines, and Bookmarks

Browsing the internet on your smartphone involves using browsers to access websites, search for information, and save your favorite sites for future reference. Understanding URLs, search engines, and bookmarks will enhance your browsing experience. Let's explore each of these aspects:

1. URLs (Uniform Resource Locators):

URLs are web addresses that identify specific locations or resources on the internet. They serve as the entry points to websites and online content. Here's how to use URLs to access websites:

Entering URLs:

- To visit a specific website, open your smartphone's web browser, tap the address bar, and type the URL of the website you want to visit (e.g., www.example.com).
- After entering the URL, press "Go" or "Enter" to load the website.

Navigating the Web:

- Within a website, URLs often change as you navigate from one page to another. You can return to the previous page by tapping the back arrow in your browser's navigation bar.

2. Search Engines:

Search engines are powerful tools that help you find information, websites, images, videos, and more on the internet. The most popular search engines are Google, Bing, Yahoo, and DuckDuckGo. Here's how to use search engines on your smartphone:

Conducting a Search:

- Open your smartphone's web browser.
- Tap the search bar at the top of the browser's screen.
- Type your search query (e.g., "best restaurants near me" or "how to bake a cake") and press "Search" or "Enter."
- The search engine will display a list of search results relevant to your query.

Refining Your Search:

- To get more specific results, you can use quotation marks to search for exact phrases (e.g., "healthy smoothie recipes") or use minus (-) to exclude certain terms (e.g., "best smartphones -iPhone").

3. Bookmarks:

Bookmarks allow you to save and easily access your favorite websites without having to remember or re-enter their URLs. Here's how to use bookmarks on your smartphone:

Adding Bookmarks:

- When you come across a website you want to save, tap the "Share" or "Options" icon in your browser.
- Select "Add to bookmarks" or "Bookmark this page."
- Choose a name for the bookmark, and it will be saved for future reference.

Accessing Bookmarks:

- To access your bookmarks, tap the bookmark icon in your browser's interface. This icon may be a star or a book symbol, depending on the browser.
- You'll see a list of your saved bookmarks. Tap on a bookmark to open the associated website.

Organizing Bookmarks:

- To keep your bookmarks organized, you can create folders and categorize them based on topics or interests.

Using URLs, search engines, and bookmarks, you can efficiently explore the web and access the information you need on your smartphone. Browsing the internet offers a vast array of knowledge and entertainment, but it's essential to stay safe online.

Staying Safe Online: Avoiding Scams and Phishing

Staying safe online is of utmost importance to protect your personal information, privacy, and digital assets. Scams and phishing are common threats on the internet, and being aware of these risks can help you avoid falling victim to them. Here's how to stay safe and protect yourself from scams and phishing attempts while using your smartphone:

1. Recognizing Scams and Phishing:

Scams:

- Scams are fraudulent schemes designed to deceive you into providing money, personal information, or access to your accounts under false pretenses.
- Common scams include fake lottery winnings, prize notifications, fake tech support, and charity scams.

Phishing:

- Phishing is a form of cyber-attack where attackers pose as trustworthy entities, such as banks, social media platforms, or government agencies, to trick you into revealing

sensitive information like usernames, passwords, or credit card details.
- Phishing attempts are often carried out through emails, messages, or websites that mimic legitimate sources.

2. Tips to Avoid Scams and Phishing:

Be Skeptical:

- Be cautious of unsolicited emails, messages, or phone calls that claim you've won a prize or need to provide personal information urgently.
- Avoid clicking on links or downloading attachments from unknown sources.

Verify the Source:

- Before providing any sensitive information, verify the sender's identity, especially if they claim to be from a reputable organization.

- Check the email address, website URL, or contact number to ensure they are genuine.

Avoid Sharing Sensitive Information:

- Legitimate organizations will never ask for sensitive information like passwords, Social Security numbers, or credit card details via email or messages.
- Avoid sharing such information through electronic communications.

Use Strong Passwords:

- Use strong, unique passwords for your online accounts and avoid using the same password for multiple sites.
- Consider using a password manager to securely store and generate complex passwords.

Keep Software Updated:

- Keep your smartphone's operating system, apps, and antivirus software up to date to protect against known vulnerabilities and security threats.

Enable Two-Factor Authentication (2FA):

- Enable 2FA whenever possible. This adds an extra layer of security by requiring a second form of verification (e.g., a one-time code sent to your phone) when logging into your accounts.

Use Secure Websites:

- When entering sensitive information or making online transactions, ensure the website URL begins with "https://" and displays a padlock symbol in the address bar. This indicates a secure connection.

Report Suspicious Activities:

- If you encounter suspicious emails, messages, or websites, report them to your email provider or the appropriate authorities.

Educate Yourself:

- Stay informed about the latest scams and phishing techniques to recognize and avoid potential threats.

Remember that staying safe online is an ongoing effort. Cybercriminals are continually evolving their tactics, so it's crucial to remain vigilant and take proactive measures to protect yourself. By being cautious, using strong security practices, and following these tips, you can have a safer and more enjoyable online experience on your smartphone.

VI. SOCIAL MEDIA 101

Introduction to Popular Social Media Platforms

Social media platforms have revolutionized the way we connect, communicate, and share information in the digital age. These platforms have become an integral part of daily life, offering various ways to interact with friends, family, and people from all around the world. Let's explore some of the most popular social media platforms:

1. **Facebook:**
    - With billions of active users, Facebook is one of the largest and most influential social media platforms globally. Users can create profiles, add friends, share posts, photos, and videos, join groups, and follow pages of their interests.
2. **Instagram:**
    - Instagram is a visually-oriented platform centered around photos and videos. Users can share images and short videos, add captions and hashtags, and

engage with others through likes, comments, and direct messages.

3. **Twitter:**
   - Twitter is a microblogging platform known for its brevity. Users can send short messages called "tweets" limited to 280 characters, follow others, retweet, and engage in conversations using hashtags.

4. **LinkedIn:**
   - LinkedIn is a professional networking platform designed for career-oriented individuals. Users can create professional profiles, connect with colleagues and potential employers, and share industry-related content.

5. **YouTube:**
   - YouTube is the largest video-sharing platform where users can upload, watch, like, and comment on videos. It hosts a wide range of content, including vlogs, educational videos, music, and more.

6. **Snapchat:**
   - Snapchat is a multimedia messaging app with a unique feature of disappearing messages and

photos. Users can send "Snaps" to friends and post content to their "Stories" that vanish after a short period.

7. **Pinterest:**
   - Pinterest is a visual discovery platform where users can find, save, and organize ideas or inspirations through images and "pins." It's particularly popular for DIY, fashion, and home décor ideas.

8. **Reddit:**
   - Reddit is a vast community-driven platform known for its "subreddits," which are topic-specific communities where users discuss various subjects, share content, and engage in discussions.

9. **TikTok:**
   - TikTok is a video-sharing app that allows users to create short, creative videos with music, filters, and special effects. It has gained immense popularity for its entertaining and viral content.

10. **WhatsApp:**
    - WhatsApp is a messaging app that enables users to send text messages, voice messages, images, and videos to contacts. It also supports voice and video calls.

Each social media platform offers unique features and caters to different audiences. They provide opportunities to express creativity, stay informed about current events, build connections, and engage with diverse communities.

As you explore these platforms, remember to be mindful of your online behavior, protect your privacy, and use them responsibly. Understanding the features and settings of each platform can help you make the most of your social media experience and create a positive digital presence.

Creating and Managing Social Media Accounts

Creating and managing social media accounts is a straightforward process that allows you to join various platforms and interact with friends, family, and communities of shared interests. Here's a step-by-step guide to help you get started:

1. Choosing a Platform:

- Determine which social media platforms align with your interests, communication preferences, and goals. Consider factors such as the type of content you want to share, the communities you wish to engage with, and your privacy preferences.

2. Account Creation:

- Download the social media app from your smartphone's app store or visit the platform's website on your smartphone's browser.
- Click on "Sign Up" or "Create Account" to begin the account creation process.

3. Providing Your Information:

- Most social media platforms will ask for certain basic information during the sign-up process. This may include your name, email address, or phone number. Some platforms might also require you to choose a username or handle.

4. Setting a Password:

- Create a strong and unique password for your social media account. Avoid using easily guessable information like your name or birthdate.

5. Verifying Your Account:

- Depending on the platform, you may need to verify your email address or phone number to complete the account creation process. This step is essential for account security and recovery.

6. Profile Setup:

- Once your account is created, take the time to set up your profile. Add a profile picture that represents you or your brand and write a bio or description that introduces yourself to other users.

7. Connecting with Others:

- Start connecting with friends, family, colleagues, or people with shared interests. You can do this by searching for their names or handles and sending them a friend or connection request.

8. Privacy Settings:

- Review the platform's privacy settings and customize them according to your preferences. You can control who can see your posts, who can send you friend requests or messages, and other privacy-related options.

9. Content Sharing:

- Begin sharing content, such as posts, photos, videos, or updates, based on your interests and what you want to share with your audience.

10. Managing Your Account: - Regularly check your notifications, messages, and friend requests to stay updated with your social media interactions. - Engage with your audience by responding to comments, messages, and mentions.

11. Account Security: - Keep your account secure by logging out when using shared devices, using strong and unique passwords, and enabling two-factor authentication whenever available.

12. Managing Multiple Accounts: - If you decide to join multiple social media platforms, consider using social media management tools or apps to manage and schedule your posts efficiently.

Remember that different social media platforms have unique features and communities. It's essential to familiarize yourself with the platform's terms of service, community guidelines, and privacy policies to ensure you use the platform responsibly and respectfully.

By creating and managing social media accounts, you can build meaningful connections, share your interests, and engage with others in the digital world.

Understanding Privacy Settings and Sharing Responsibly

Understanding privacy settings and sharing responsibly is crucial for maintaining control over your online presence and protecting your personal information. Social media platforms offer various privacy features that allow you to control who can see your posts and interact with you. Here are some essential tips for understanding privacy settings and practicing responsible sharing on social media:

1. Review Privacy Settings:

- Take the time to explore and understand the privacy settings of each social media platform you use. These settings can usually be found in the account or settings section.
- Customize your privacy preferences to control who can see your posts, who can send you friend requests, and who can message you.

2. Choose Your Audience:

- Decide whether you want your posts to be visible to the public, friends only, or a select group of people. Most platforms offer options to customize the audience for each post.

3. Be Cautious About Personal Information:

- Avoid sharing sensitive personal information, such as your address, phone number, financial details, or travel plans, publicly on social media.
- Consider sharing personal information through private messages or with a limited circle of trusted friends.

4. Use Strong Passwords:

- Set strong and unique passwords for your social media accounts. Avoid using easily guessable information like your name, birthdate, or common words.

- Enable two-factor authentication whenever possible to add an extra layer of security to your accounts.

5. Think Before You Post:

- Be mindful of the content you share on social media. Once something is posted, it may be challenging to remove it entirely from the internet.
- Consider how your posts might be perceived by others and how they may impact your personal or professional reputation.

6. Respect Others' Privacy:

- Obtain consent before posting or tagging others in photos, videos, or location check-ins.
- Be respectful of others' privacy preferences, and avoid sharing sensitive information about them without their permission.

7. Avoid Oversharing:

- While sharing updates about your life can be enjoyable, avoid oversharing personal or intimate details that could be better kept private.

8. Be Mindful of Location Sharing:

- Be cautious about sharing your real-time location on social media. Some platforms allow you to disable location tagging in posts to protect your privacy.

9. Review and Adjust Settings Regularly:

- Periodically review your privacy settings and update them as needed based on changes in your preferences or circumstances.

10. Report Inappropriate Content: - If you come across content that violates community guidelines or appears to be harmful, report it to the platform administrators.

By understanding and utilizing privacy settings effectively, you can manage your online presence and limit the visibility of your posts to those you trust. Sharing responsibly helps protect your personal information and promotes a positive and safe online environment for you and others.

VII. MASTERING MESSAGING APPS

Using WhatsApp, Messenger and Other Messaging Platforms

Using messaging platforms like WhatsApp, Messenger, and other similar apps is a straightforward and convenient way to communicate with friends, family, and colleagues. These apps offer a wide range of features to enhance your messaging experience. Here's a detailed guide on how to use WhatsApp, Messenger, and other messaging platforms effectively:

WhatsApp:

1. Sending Messages:

- Open WhatsApp and select the chat of the contact you want to message.
- Type your message in the text box at the bottom of the screen.

- Tap the send button (usually a paper plane icon) to send the message.

2. Sending Photos, Videos, and Voice Messages:

- To send a photo or video, tap the attachment icon (paperclip or "+" symbol) within the chat, choose "Gallery," select the media, and tap send.
- To send a voice message, hold down the microphone icon to record, then release to send.

3. Making Voice and Video Calls:

- To make a voice call, open the chat with the contact, tap the phone icon at the top right corner of the screen, and wait for the recipient to answer.
- To make a video call, tap the video camera icon at the top right corner of the screen.

4. Creating Group Chats:

- In WhatsApp, you can create group chats by tapping the three-dot menu, selecting "New group," and adding contacts to the group.

Facebook Messenger:

1. Sending Messages:

- Open Messenger and select the chat of the person you want to message.
- Type your message in the text box at the bottom of the screen.
- Tap the send button (usually a paper plane icon) to send the message.

2. Sending Photos, Videos, and Voice Messages:

- To send a photo or video, tap the camera icon within the chat, choose "Photo/Video," select the media, and tap send.

- To send a voice message, hold down the microphone icon to record, then release to send.

3. Making Voice and Video Calls:

- To make a voice call, open the chat with the contact, tap the phone icon at the top right corner of the screen, and wait for the recipient to answer.
- To make a video call, tap the video camera icon at the top right corner of the screen.

Other Messaging Platforms:

The steps for using other messaging platforms are generally similar to WhatsApp and Messenger. Here's a general guide for using most messaging apps:

1. Sending Messages:

- Open the messaging app and select the chat of the person you want to message.

- Type your message in the text box at the bottom of the screen.
- Tap the send button to send the message.

2. Sending Photos, Videos, and Voice Messages:

- To send a photo or video, tap the attachment or camera icon within the chat, choose "Gallery" or "Camera," select the media, and tap send.
- To send a voice message, hold down the microphone icon to record, then release to send.

3. Making Voice and Video Calls:

- To make a voice call, open the chat with the contact, tap the phone icon or call button, and wait for the recipient to answer.
- To make a video call, tap the video camera icon or video call button.

4. Creating Group Chats:

- In most messaging apps, you can create group chats by tapping the menu or options button, selecting "New group," and adding contacts to the group.

Using messaging platforms is an efficient way to keep in touch with others, share media, and have voice or video conversations. Remember to respect others' privacy, and be mindful of the information you share on these platforms.

Sending Photos, Videos and Voice Messages

Sending photos, videos, and voice messages is a common and enjoyable way to share experiences and communicate with friends and family through messaging platforms. Here's a step-by-step guide on how to send these types of media using messaging apps like WhatsApp, Messenger, and other similar platforms:

1. Sending Photos:

On WhatsApp:

- Open the chat with the contact you want to send the photo to.
- Tap the attachment icon (paperclip) or the "+" symbol.
- Choose "Gallery" to access your phone's photo gallery.
- Select the photo you want to send.
- Optionally, you can add a caption or message to accompany the photo.
- Tap the send button (usually a paper plane icon) to send the photo.

On Facebook Messenger:

- Open the chat with the person you want to send the photo to.
- Tap the camera icon or the "+" symbol.
- Choose "Photo/Video."
- Select the photo you want to send.
- Optionally, you can add a caption or message to accompany the photo.
- Tap the send button to send the photo.

2. Sending Videos:

On WhatsApp:

- Follow the same steps as sending photos, but instead of selecting a photo, choose a video from your gallery.

On Facebook Messenger:

- Follow the same steps as sending photos, but instead of selecting a photo, choose a video from your gallery.

3. Sending Voice Messages:

On WhatsApp:

- Open the chat with the contact you want to send the voice message to.
- Tap and hold the microphone icon (located to the right of the text input box).
- Start speaking your message while holding down the microphone icon.
- Release the microphone icon when you're done recording the message.
- The voice message will be automatically sent once you release the microphone icon.

On Facebook Messenger:

- Open the chat with the person you want to send the voice message to.
- Tap and hold the microphone icon (located to the right of the text input box).
- Start speaking your message while holding down the microphone icon.

- Release the microphone icon when you're done recording the message.
- The voice message will be automatically sent once you release the microphone icon.

4. Sending Multiple Photos or Videos:

In both WhatsApp and Facebook Messenger, you can send multiple photos or videos at once by selecting multiple media files from your gallery before tapping the send button. This is especially useful when you want to share a collection of photos or a series of short videos.

Remember to be mindful of the file size when sending media, as larger files may take longer to upload and send, and they might consume more data if you're not using a Wi-Fi connection.

By using these features, you can easily share your visual experiences and voice messages, making your conversations more engaging and expressive.

Making Voice and Video Calls Through Messaging Apps

Making voice and video calls through messaging apps allows you to have real-time conversations with your contacts, whether they are across the street or around the world. Here's how to make voice and video calls using popular messaging platforms like WhatsApp, Messenger, and others:

1. Making Voice Calls:

On WhatsApp:

- Open the chat with the contact you want to call.
- Look for the phone icon at the top right corner of the screen.
- Tap the phone icon to initiate the voice call.
- Wait for the recipient to answer the call.

On Facebook Messenger:

- Open the chat with the person you want to call.
- Look for the phone icon at the top right corner of the screen.
- Tap the phone icon to initiate the voice call.

- Wait for the recipient to answer the call.

On Other Messaging Platforms:

- The process of making voice calls is usually similar across various messaging apps.
- Look for the phone or call icon within the chat screen.
- Tap the icon to initiate the voice call.
- Wait for the recipient to answer the call.

2. Making Video Calls:

On WhatsApp:

- Open the chat with the contact you want to call.
- Look for the video camera icon at the top right corner of the screen.
- Tap the video camera icon to initiate the video call.
- Wait for the recipient to answer the call.

On Facebook Messenger:

- Open the chat with the person you want to call.
- Look for the video camera icon at the top right corner of the screen.
- Tap the video camera icon to initiate the video call.
- Wait for the recipient to answer the call.

On Other Messaging Platforms:

- The process of making video calls is usually similar across various messaging apps.
- Look for the video camera or video call icon within the chat screen.
- Tap the icon to initiate the video call.
- Wait for the recipient to answer the call.

3. Group Voice and Video Calls:

Many messaging apps also support group voice and video calls, allowing you to connect with multiple contacts simultaneously:

On WhatsApp:

- Open the group chat you want to call.
- Look for the phone or video camera icon at the top right corner of the screen.
- Tap the icon to initiate the group voice or video call.
- Wait for the participants to answer the call.

On Facebook Messenger:

- Open the group chat you want to call.
- Look for the phone or video camera icon at the top right corner of the screen.
- Tap the icon to initiate the group voice or video call.
- Wait for the participants to answer the call.

On Other Messaging Platforms:

- The process of making group voice and video calls may vary slightly across different apps, but it's typically similar to initiating one-on-one calls.

- Look for the relevant icons within the group chat and tap to initiate the call.
- Wait for the participants to answer the call.

By using the voice and video call features on messaging apps, you can have more personal and engaging conversations with your contacts. Enjoy the convenience of staying connected and sharing special moments in real time.

VIII. COMPUTERS MADE EASY

Introduction to Desktops, Laptops and Operating Systems

In the digital age, computers have become an integral part of our daily lives, enabling us to work, communicate, and access information with ease. Understanding the basics of desktops, laptops, and operating systems is essential for harnessing the full potential of these powerful devices. Let's explore each of these components:

Desktop Computers:

- A desktop computer is a stationary device designed to be used on a desk or table. It typically consists of a computer case (CPU), a monitor, a keyboard, and a mouse. Desktops offer powerful processing capabilities and are often preferred for tasks that demand high performance, such as graphic design, video editing, and gaming. They usually provide ample storage space and are more customizable, allowing users to upgrade hardware components easily.

Laptop Computers:

- A laptop, also known as a notebook, is a portable computer designed for on-the-go use. Unlike desktops, laptops integrate all essential components into a single unit, including the monitor, keyboard, and trackpad or touchpad. Some models also include a touchscreen feature. Laptops are versatile and suitable for a wide range of tasks, making them a popular choice for work, entertainment, and general computing needs.

Operating Systems:

- An operating system (OS) is a software that manages computer hardware and software resources and acts as an intermediary between the user and the computer's hardware. It provides a user-friendly interface, enabling users to interact with the computer and run applications. Operating systems handle tasks such as memory management, file management, and device drivers. The most commonly used operating systems are:

- **Windows:** Developed by Microsoft, Windows is one of the most popular operating systems for desktop and laptop computers. It provides a familiar user interface with a Start Menu, taskbar, and desktop icons. Windows supports a vast array of software applications and is compatible with a wide range of hardware.

- **macOS:** Developed by Apple, macOS is the operating system exclusive to Apple's Mac computers. Known for its sleek design and seamless integration with Apple hardware, macOS offers a user-friendly interface and numerous built-in applications. It is widely used in creative industries and is favored by many for its performance and security features.

- **Linux:** Linux is an open-source operating system that comes in various distributions (distros). It is popular among developers, tech enthusiasts, and those seeking customization options. Linux is known for its stability, security, and ability to run on a wide range of hardware configurations.

Understanding the differences between desktops and laptops, as well as the features and advantages of various operating systems, allows you to make informed decisions when choosing the right computer for your needs. Whether you opt for a powerful desktop or the portability of a laptop, the operating system you select plays a crucial role in determining your computing experience.

Navigating the Desktop: Icons, Taskbar and Start Menu

Navigating the desktop involves mastering the essential elements that make up the graphical user interface (GUI) of your computer. Whether you are using Windows or macOS, understanding icons, the taskbar (Windows) or dock (macOS), and the Start Menu (Windows) or Finder (macOS) is fundamental for efficient computer usage.

Icons: Icons are graphical representations of applications, files, or folders. They are displayed on your desktop and provide quick access to various programs and documents. Here's how to work with icons:

On Windows:

- To open a program or file, double-click its icon on the desktop.
- To move an icon, click and hold it, then drag it to a new location on the desktop.
- To delete an icon, right-click it and select "Delete."

On macOS:

- To open an application or file, double-click its icon on the desktop.
- To move an icon, click and hold it, then drag it to a new location on the desktop.
- To delete an icon, click it once and press the "Delete" key on your keyboard, or drag it to the trash bin on the dock.

Taskbar (Windows) / Dock (macOS): The taskbar (Windows) or dock (macOS) is a convenient and accessible area that provides quick access to frequently used applications and system functions. Here's how to use them:

On Windows:

- The taskbar is typically located at the bottom of the screen.
- Pin your favorite applications to the taskbar for easy access. Right-click an application and select "Pin to taskbar."
- Open applications will display their icons on the taskbar, making it easy to switch between them.

On macOS:

- The dock is usually located at the bottom of the screen.
- Drag applications to the dock for quick access. Alternatively, right-click an application and select "Options" > "Keep in Dock."
- Open applications will display their icons on the dock, allowing you to switch between them easily.

Start Menu (Windows) / Finder (macOS): The Start Menu (Windows) or Finder (macOS) serves as the main hub for accessing programs, files, and settings. Here's how to use them:

On Windows:

- Click the "Start" button on the taskbar to open the Start Menu.
- Use the search bar to quickly find and launch applications, settings, and files.
- Browse through the installed applications and access system functions, such as the control panel and power options.

On macOS:

- Click the Finder icon on the dock to open Finder.
- Use Spotlight (the magnifying glass icon in the top-right corner) to search for applications, files, and other content.
- Access commonly used folders, files, and system settings from the Finder sidebar.

Mastering these navigation elements allows you to efficiently use your computer, launch applications, and access files with ease.

Using Files and Folders: Creating, Organizing and Searching

Using files and folders effectively is essential for organizing and managing your digital content on your computer. It allows for easy access to documents, media files, and other data, making your computing experience more efficient.

Creating Files and Folders:

On Windows:

- To create a new file, right-click on an empty area on the desktop or inside a folder, hover over "New," and select the file type you want to create (e.g., Text Document, Microsoft Word Document).
- To create a new folder, right-click on an empty area on the desktop or inside a folder, hover over "New," and choose "Folder."

On macOS:

- To create a new file, right-click on an empty area on the desktop or inside a folder, hover over "New Folder with

Selection," and select the file type you want to create (e.g., New Text Document, New Folder).
- To create a new folder, right-click on an empty area on the desktop or inside a folder, select "New Folder."

Organizing Files and Folders:

On Windows:

- To organize files and folders, drag and drop them into the desired location.
- Create subfolders to categorize related files and keep your data organized.
- Use descriptive names for files and folders to quickly identify their contents.

On macOS:

- To organize files and folders, drag and drop them into the desired location.
- Use Finder tags and color labels to categorize files and easily find them later.

- Create smart folders that automatically gather files based on specific criteria, such as file type or creation date.

Searching for Files:

On Windows:

- Use the search bar located in the taskbar to search for files, applications, and settings by typing keywords.
- The search results will display relevant files and folders that match your search query.

On macOS:

- Use Spotlight, the magnifying glass icon in the top-right corner of the menu bar, to search for files, applications, and other content by typing keywords.
- Spotlight provides instant search results and can also perform calculations, look up definitions, and more.

Advanced Search Options (Both Windows and macOS):

- Use advanced search options to narrow down your search results based on file type, date modified, file size, and other criteria.
- In Windows, click on "Search Tools" to access advanced search options. In macOS, click on "Show All in Finder" to reveal additional search filters.

By creating folders and organizing your files thoughtfully, you can keep your data well-structured and accessible. Utilizing the search capabilities of your operating system allows for quick retrieval of specific files and information, saving you time and effort.

IX. INTERNET AND EMAIL BASICS

Accessing the Internet and Browsing with Browsers

Accessing the internet and browsing with web browsers is a fundamental skill for using computers and exploring the vast world of online information. Web browsers allow you to visit websites, access online services, and interact with digital content. Let's dive into the steps for accessing the internet and browsing with browsers:

1. Internet Connection:

- Ensure that your computer is connected to the internet. You can connect via a wired Ethernet connection or a wireless Wi-Fi network.

2. Choose a Web Browser:

- Web browsers are software applications designed for accessing the internet. Some popular web browsers include:
    - Google Chrome: Developed by Google, Chrome is known for its speed and simplicity. It supports a vast array of extensions and is widely used worldwide.
    - Mozilla Firefox: Firefox is an open-source browser that emphasizes privacy and customization. It offers a range of add-ons to enhance the browsing experience.
    - Microsoft Edge: Formerly Internet Explorer, Microsoft Edge is the default browser on Windows devices. It offers smooth integration with Windows features.
    - Safari: Safari is the default browser on macOS and is optimized for Apple devices, providing excellent performance and energy efficiency.

3. Launch the Web Browser:

- Locate the web browser icon on your desktop or in your computer's applications folder.
- Double-click the icon to open the web browser.

4. Navigate to Websites:

- In the address bar at the top of the browser window, type the URL (web address) of the website you want to visit (e.g., www.example.com).
- Press Enter or Return on your keyboard to load the website.

5. Interacting with Webpages:

- Once the website loads, you can interact with its content.
- Click on links to navigate to other pages within the same website or external sites.
- Use the back and forward buttons on the browser to move between previously visited pages.

6. Search Engines:

- If you don't know the exact website address, you can use search engines like Google (www.google.com) or Bing (www.bing.com) to find information. Type keywords related to your query in the search bar, and press Enter to view the search results.

7. Tabs and Windows:

- Browsers support multiple tabs and windows, allowing you to have several webpages open simultaneously. To open a new tab, click the "+" icon on the browser's tab bar. To open a new window, go to the menu and select "New Window."

8. Bookmarks (Favorites):

- Save frequently visited websites as bookmarks (favorites) to quickly access them later. Click the star icon in the browser's address bar to bookmark the current page.

Mastering web browsing skills will empower you to explore the internet, access information, and utilize online services.

Setting Up and Using Email Accounts

Setting up and using email accounts is a fundamental aspect of modern communication. Email (electronic mail) allows you to send and receive digital messages, documents, and media files to and from anyone around the world. Here's a step-by-step guide on how to set up and use an email account:

1. Choose an Email Service Provider:

- Select an email service provider that suits your needs. Some popular providers include Gmail (by Google), Outlook (by Microsoft), Yahoo Mail, and iCloud Mail (by Apple).

2. Sign Up for an Email Account:

- Go to the website of your chosen email service provider (e.g., www.gmail.com, www.outlook.com).
- Click on the "Sign Up" or "Create Account" button.
- Provide the required information, such as your name, desired email address, password, and recovery options (phone number or alternative email).

- Agree to the terms of service and privacy policy, and complete the sign-up process.

3. Verify Your Account:

- After signing up, you may need to verify your account. This can be done by clicking on a link sent to your alternative email address or by entering a verification code sent to your phone number.

4. Log In to Your Email Account:

- Go to the website of your email service provider.
- Click on the "Sign In" or "Log In" button.
- Enter your email address and password.
- Click on the "Sign In" or "Log In" button to access your email account.

5. Compose and Send an Email:

- Click on the "Compose" or "New" button to start a new email.
- In the "To" field, enter the recipient's email address.
- Add a subject to the email in the "Subject" field.
- Compose your message in the main body of the email.
- Click on the "Send" button to send the email.

6. Receive and Read Emails:

- When someone sends you an email, it will appear in your inbox.
- Click on an email to open and read its contents.

7. Organize Your Emails:

- Use folders or labels to organize your emails (e.g., Inbox, Sent, Drafts, Archive, etc.).
- Mark important emails as "Starred" or "Flagged" for easy retrieval.

- Delete unwanted emails to keep your inbox clutter-free.

8. Customize Your Email Account:

- Explore the settings of your email account to customize your experience. You can set a signature, change the theme, manage notifications, and more.

Using email accounts efficiently can greatly improve your communication and productivity. It allows you to stay connected with friends, family, colleagues, and business partners.

Sending, Receiving and Managing Emails

Sending, receiving, and managing emails efficiently is essential for effective communication and staying organized in your digital correspondence. Let's explore the steps for sending, receiving, and managing emails:

Sending Emails:

1. **Compose a New Email:**
    - Click on the "Compose" or "New" button (the exact wording may vary depending on the email service provider) to start writing a new email.
2. **Recipient(s):**
    - Enter the recipient's email address in the "To" field. If you are sending the email to multiple recipients, separate their email addresses with commas.
3. **Subject:**
    - Add a concise and informative subject in the "Subject" field. This helps the recipient understand the purpose of the email.

4. **Compose the Message:**
    - Write your email in the main body of the message window. You can use formatting options like bold, italic, and bullet points to structure your content.
5. **Attachments (Optional):**
    - If you want to attach files, such as documents or images, look for the "Attach" or "Attach Files" button. Click on it to select the files you want to attach.
6. **Review and Send:**
    - Before sending the email, review its content and attachments to ensure accuracy. Once you are satisfied, click the "Send" button to dispatch the email to the recipient(s).

Receiving Emails:

1. **Inbox:**
    - When someone sends you an email, it will appear in your inbox—the primary folder for incoming emails.
2. **Open and Read Emails:**

- To read an email, click on its subject in your inbox. The email's content will open in a new window or tab.

3. **Replying to Emails:**
   - To reply to an email, click on the "Reply" button in the email window. A reply message will open, and you can compose your response.

4. **Forwarding Emails:**
   - To forward an email to someone else, click on the "Forward" button in the email window. Enter the recipient's email address and add any additional comments if needed.

Managing Emails:

1. **Folders or Labels:**
   - Organize your emails by creating folders (or labels) to categorize them based on topics or projects. For example, you can have folders for Work, Personal, Travel, etc. Drag and drop emails into the appropriate folders for better organization.

2. **Marking Emails as Important:**
   - Use the "Star" or "Flag" feature to mark important emails that require your attention or follow-up.
3. **Deleting Emails:**
   - Delete unwanted emails to keep your inbox clean and clutter-free. You can usually find a "Delete" button or icon in the email interface.
4. **Search and Filters:**
   - Use the search bar to find specific emails by entering keywords, sender's name, or subject. Many email services also offer filtering options to organize emails automatically based on criteria you set.

By effectively sending, receiving, and managing emails, you can stay on top of your digital communication and maintain a well-organized inbox.

X. TROUBLESHOOTING TIPS

Common Smartphone and Computer Issues and How to Fix Them

As convenient as smartphones and computers are, they can occasionally encounter technical issues. Understanding common problems and their solutions empowers you to resolve them quickly. Here are some typical smartphone and computer issues and how to fix them.

Smartphone Issues:

1. **Battery Drain:**
    - Close unnecessary apps running in the background.
    - Lower screen brightness or enable power-saving mode.
    - Turn off features like Bluetooth, Wi-Fi, and location services when not in use.
2. **Overheating:**
    - Close resource-intensive apps or games.

- Remove the phone's case to improve heat dissipation.
- Avoid exposing the phone to direct sunlight or hot environments.

3. **Slow Performance:**
   - Clear cache and temporary files to free up storage.
   - Uninstall unused apps to free up memory.
   - Restart your phone to refresh system processes.

4. **Unresponsive Touchscreen:**
   - Clean the screen with a soft, lint-free cloth.
   - Remove screen protectors or cases that may interfere with touch sensitivity.
   - Restart the phone to resolve temporary glitches.

5. **App Crashes:**
   - Update the app to the latest version from the app store.
   - Clear app cache or data in the device settings.
   - Reinstall the app if the issue persists.

Computer Issues:

1. **Slow Performance:**
    - Close unnecessary programs and browser tabs.
    - Run a disk cleanup to remove temporary files.
    - Upgrade hardware components like RAM or SSD for better performance.
2. **Blue Screen of Death (BSOD) on Windows:**
    - Restart the computer to see if it was a temporary error.
    - Check for driver updates or software conflicts.
    - Run Windows' built-in troubleshooting tools.
3. **Internet Connectivity Issues:**
    - Check if other devices can connect to the internet.
    - Reset the router or modem.
    - Update network drivers or troubleshoot network settings.
4. **Freezing or Hanging:**
    - Check for software updates and install them.
    - Run a malware scan to ensure the system is clean.
    - Check for overheating and clean the computer's interior if necessary.

5. **No Sound or Audio Issues:**
    - Check the volume settings and ensure speakers or headphones are properly connected.
    - Update audio drivers from the manufacturer's website.
    - Check the Windows or macOS audio settings for any issues.

Remember that some issues may require advanced troubleshooting, and it's essential to back up your data before attempting any major fixes. If you are unsure how to resolve a problem, it's always a good idea to seek help from technical support or an experienced professional.

When and Where to Seek Technical Support

Knowing when and where to seek technical support is crucial for resolving complex issues and ensuring the optimal performance of your devices. Here are some scenarios when you should seek technical support and the places where you can find assistance:

1. Device Malfunction or Hardware Issues:

- When your smartphone or computer experiences a hardware-related problem, such as a non-functional screen, battery issues, or connectivity problems, it's best to seek support from the manufacturer or authorized service centers.

2. Software Errors and Glitches:

- If your device is encountering software-related issues like crashes, freezes, or error messages, you can seek help from the following sources:
    - **Official Support Websites:** Many manufacturers and software developers offer support resources on

their official websites, including FAQs, troubleshooting guides, and forums.
- **Online Tech Forums and Communities:** Participate in tech forums or communities where experienced users and experts can provide guidance and solutions to common software problems.

3. Network Connectivity and Internet Issues:

- If you experience problems with your internet connection, reach out to your internet service provider (ISP) for assistance. They can help diagnose connectivity issues or perform remote troubleshooting.

4. Email and Account Support:

- For issues related to your email accounts, such as login problems, password recovery, or email delivery problems, you can seek help from your email service provider's customer support.

5. Software Updates and Security:

- Keep your devices and software up-to-date to prevent security vulnerabilities. Regularly check for updates on the device manufacturer's website or within the software settings.

6. Online Purchases and Transactions:

- If you encounter issues with online purchases or transactions, contact the customer support of the specific website or platform where the transaction occurred.

7. General Technical Assistance:

- If you are facing a technical issue that you cannot resolve on your own, consider seeking help from professional technical support services or local IT experts.

8. Maintenance and Regular Checkups:

- Consider scheduling regular maintenance checkups for your devices, especially for computers. IT professionals can help optimize performance, remove malware, and ensure your devices are in good working condition.

Remember, while troubleshooting common issues can often be done independently, seeking technical support becomes necessary when encountering more complex or hardware-related problems. It's always essential to back up your data before seeking assistance to prevent data loss during troubleshooting or repairs.

Maintaining the Performance and Security of Devices

Maintaining the performance and security of your devices is crucial to ensure they function optimally and protect your data from potential threats. Here are essential tips to help you keep your smartphones and computers in top-notch condition:

1. Regular Software Updates:

- Keep your operating systems, apps, and security software up-to-date. Software updates often include bug fixes, performance improvements, and security patches.

2. Use Trusted Antivirus and Antimalware Software:

- Install reputable antivirus and antimalware programs to protect your devices from viruses, malware, and other malicious threats. Keep these security programs updated for the best protection.

3. Strong Passwords and Two-Factor Authentication:

- Use strong and unique passwords for your accounts and devices. Consider enabling two-factor authentication (2FA) whenever possible for an extra layer of security.

4. Back Up Your Data Regularly:

- Regularly back up your important files, documents, photos, and other data to an external hard drive, cloud storage, or a secure backup service. This ensures you can recover your data in case of data loss or device failure.

5. Be Cautious with Email and Downloads:

- Avoid opening email attachments or clicking on links from unknown or suspicious sources. Be cautious when downloading software from unofficial websites, as it may contain malware.

6. Clear Cache and Temporary Files:

- Regularly clear cache and temporary files from your devices. Accumulated cache can slow down your device's performance over time.

7. Manage Startup Programs:

- Disable unnecessary programs from launching at startup. This helps speed up your computer's boot time and improves overall performance.

8. Monitor Storage Space:

- Keep an eye on your device's storage space. Delete unused files and apps to free up space and prevent performance issues.

9. Manage Browser Extensions:

- Periodically review and remove unnecessary browser extensions. Too many extensions can slow down your browser's performance.

10. Secure Your Network:

- Protect your Wi-Fi network with a strong password and encryption. Use WPA2 or WPA3 security protocols for wireless networks.

11. Use a Firewall:

- Enable the built-in firewall on your computer to help prevent unauthorized access and block malicious network traffic.

12. Avoid Public Wi-Fi:

- Be cautious when using public Wi-Fi networks. Avoid accessing sensitive information or making financial transactions on unsecured networks.

13. Enable Find My Device (Smartphones):

- Enable the Find My Device feature on your smartphone. This helps you locate, lock, or erase your device if it gets lost or stolen.

By following these maintenance and security practices, you can significantly enhance the performance, longevity, and safety of your smartphones and computers.

XI. STAYING SAFE AND SECURE

Protecting Devices with Passwords and Biometrics

Protecting your devices with passwords and biometrics is a crucial step in ensuring the security of your personal information and data. Here's how you can use passwords and biometrics effectively to safeguard your devices:

1. Strong Passwords:

- Create strong passwords for each of your devices. A strong password should be a combination of letters (both uppercase and lowercase), numbers, and special characters.
- Avoid using easily guessable information such as birthdays, names, or common words in your passwords.
- Use a different password for each device and online account to prevent a security breach on one account from affecting others.

2. Biometric Authentication:

- If your device supports biometric authentication (fingerprint, facial recognition, or iris scan), consider enabling it for added security.
- Biometrics provide a convenient and secure way to unlock your device, as they are unique to you and difficult to replicate.

3. Use PIN or Pattern Lock:

- If your device does not have biometric authentication, use a PIN or pattern lock to secure it.
- Choose a PIN that is not easily guessable and avoid using common sequences like "1234" or "0000."
- When using a pattern lock, create a complex pattern that is not easy to guess or observe.

4. Lock Screen Timeout:

- Set your device's lock screen to activate after a short period of inactivity. This ensures that your device locks automatically when not in use, reducing the risk of unauthorized access.

5. Avoid Sharing Passwords:

- Never share your passwords, PINs, or pattern locks with anyone, even with trusted friends or family members.
- If someone else needs access to your device, consider using a guest account or temporary access.

6. Password Managers:

- Consider using a password manager to securely store and generate complex passwords for your accounts and devices.
- Password managers help you remember unique passwords without compromising security.

7. Remote Wipe or Lock:

- Many devices offer a remote wipe or lock feature. In case your device gets lost or stolen, you can remotely erase its data or lock it to prevent unauthorized access.

8. Update Security Settings:

- Regularly review and update your device's security settings to take advantage of the latest security features and enhancements.

9. Privacy Screen Protectors:

- Consider using privacy screen protectors for your devices to prevent others from viewing your screen from angles outside your direct line of sight.

Understanding Antivirus and Security Software

Understanding antivirus and security software is essential for protecting your devices from various online threats, such as viruses, malware, spyware, and phishing attempts. Here's a breakdown of antivirus and security software and their roles in safeguarding your devices:

Antivirus Software:

Antivirus software, also known as anti-malware software, is designed to detect, prevent, and remove malicious software (malware) from your computer or smartphone. This software continuously scans your device for potential threats and takes action to neutralize or quarantine suspicious files.

Functions of Antivirus Software:

1. **Virus Detection:** Antivirus software scans files, programs, and the entire system for known viruses and malware. It uses a database of virus definitions to identify malicious code.

2. **Real-Time Protection:** Most modern antivirus programs offer real-time protection, meaning they monitor your device's activities in real-time to detect and block threats as they occur.
3. **Scheduled Scans:** Antivirus software allows you to schedule regular system scans, ensuring comprehensive and timely checks for malware.
4. **Automatic Updates:** Antivirus programs regularly update their virus definitions to stay up-to-date with the latest threats and vulnerabilities.
5. **Quarantine and Removal:** When a threat is detected, the antivirus software may quarantine the infected file or remove the malware from your device.

Firewalls:

A firewall is a security system that acts as a barrier between your device and the internet or other networks. It monitors incoming and outgoing network traffic and applies a set of rules to block unauthorized access and potentially malicious data packets.

Functions of Firewalls:

1. **Network Traffic Monitoring:** Firewalls inspect data packets traveling to and from your device to identify suspicious or unauthorized activity.
2. **Port Blocking:** Firewalls can block specific network ports to prevent unauthorized access to certain services running on your device.
3. **Intrusion Prevention:** Some firewalls have intrusion prevention capabilities that detect and block attempted intrusions from external sources.

Integrated Security Suites:

Many security software providers offer comprehensive security suites that include antivirus, firewall, antimalware, and other security features in a single package. These suites offer a complete and integrated solution to protect your devices from a wide range of threats.

Choosing Antivirus and Security Software:

When choosing antivirus and security software, consider the following factors:

1. **Reputation:** Opt for reputable and well-established security software vendors known for their reliable protection.
2. **Features:** Look for software that includes real-time protection, automatic updates, and regular system scans.
3. **Compatibility:** Ensure the software is compatible with your device's operating system.
4. **Performance Impact:** Choose software that does not significantly slow down your device's performance.

By using antivirus and security software, along with following safe online practices, you can significantly enhance your device's security and protect your personal information from cyber threats.

Best Practices for Safeguarding Personal Information

Safeguarding personal information is crucial in the digital age, where online threats and privacy concerns are prevalent. Implement these best practices to protect your sensitive data and maintain a secure digital presence:

1. Use Strong and Unique Passwords:

- Create strong passwords for all your accounts, devices, and online services. Avoid using easily guessable information like birthdays or common words.
- Use a mix of uppercase and lowercase letters, numbers, and special characters in your passwords.
- Use a password manager to securely store and generate complex passwords for each account.

2. Enable Two-Factor Authentication (2FA):

- Enable 2FA whenever possible for an extra layer of security. 2FA requires a second form of verification, such as a one-time code sent to your phone, in addition to your password.

3. Be Cautious with Emails and Links:

- Be wary of unsolicited emails and avoid clicking on links or downloading attachments from unknown sources.
- Verify the sender's email address and look for signs of phishing attempts, such as misspellings or suspicious URLs.

4. Keep Software and Devices Updated:

- Regularly update your operating systems, apps, and security software to patch vulnerabilities and stay protected against known threats.

5. Secure Your Wi-Fi Network:

- Protect your home Wi-Fi network with a strong password and encryption (WPA2 or WPA3).
- Avoid using open or public Wi-Fi for sensitive activities like online banking or accessing personal accounts.

6. Be Mindful of Social Media Privacy Settings:

- Review and adjust your social media privacy settings to control who can see your posts, personal information, and friend lists.

7. Avoid Oversharing Personal Information:

- Be cautious about sharing sensitive information on social media, public forums, or unsecured websites.

8. Securely Dispose of Devices and Data:

- Before discarding or selling old devices, ensure all data is securely wiped. Perform a factory reset or use data erasing software.
- Shred physical documents containing personal information before disposing of them.
-

9. Regularly Monitor Financial and Online Accounts:

- Monitor your financial accounts and review statements regularly for any unauthorized transactions.
- Keep track of your online accounts and be aware of any suspicious activity.

10. Use Secure Payment Methods:

- When making online purchases, use secure payment methods like credit cards or reputable payment services.

11. Back Up Important Data:

- Regularly back up your important files and data to an external drive or cloud storage to prevent data loss due to device failure or cyberattacks.

12. Educate Yourself on Cybersecurity Best Practices:

- Stay informed about the latest cybersecurity threats and best practices for staying safe online.

By following these best practices, you can significantly reduce the risk of falling victim to cyber threats, identity theft, and data breaches.

XII. BEYOND BASICS: FUN AND PRODUCTIVITY

Exploring Advanced Features and Tools

Exploring advanced features and tools on your smartphones and computers can unlock new capabilities and enhance your overall digital experience. Here are some exciting advanced features and tools to explore:

Smartphones:

1. **Manual Camera Settings:**
    - Take control of your smartphone's camera by adjusting settings like ISO, shutter speed, and white balance for more professional-looking photos.
2. **Night Mode and Low-Light Photography:**
    - Explore night mode and low-light photography features on your smartphone to capture stunning images in challenging lighting conditions.

3. **Pro Mode for Video Recording:**
   - Use the pro mode in your smartphone's video recording to adjust settings like exposure, focus, and frame rate for high-quality videos.
4. **AR (Augmented Reality) Emojis and Filters:**
   - Have fun with AR emojis and filters that allow you to transform yourself into various characters or apply creative effects to your photos and videos.
5. **Split-Screen Multitasking:**
   - On devices that support it, use split-screen multitasking to run two apps side by side, enhancing your productivity and multitasking capabilities.

Computers:

1. **Virtual Desktops:**
   - Explore virtual desktops on your computer (e.g., Windows 10 Task View or macOS Spaces) to create

separate workspaces for different tasks, increasing organization and efficiency.

2. **Keyboard Shortcuts:**
   - Master useful keyboard shortcuts for common actions like copy, paste, undo, and switching between open windows, which can save time and boost productivity.

3. **Advanced Video Editing Software:**
   - Dive into advanced video editing software like Adobe Premiere Pro or Final Cut Pro to edit and enhance your videos with professional-level tools.

4. **Graphics Design Tools:**
   - Experiment with graphics design tools such as Adobe Photoshop or Canva to create stunning visuals and graphics for personal or professional use.

Cross-Platform Features:

1. **Cloud Synchronization:**
   - Use cloud storage services like Google Drive, OneDrive, or Dropbox to sync files and data across

your devices, ensuring seamless access from anywhere.

2. **Cross-Device Continuity:**
   - Explore cross-device continuity features that allow you to start a task on one device and continue it on another, such as Handoff (macOS and iOS) or Microsoft's Continue on PC (Windows and Android).

3. **Voice Control and Voice Assistants:**
   - Embrace voice control and virtual assistants like Siri, Google Assistant, or Cortana to perform tasks, set reminders, or control devices using voice commands.

4. **Automation and Scripting:**
   - Advanced users can delve into automation tools like IFTTT, Tasker (Android), or Automator (macOS) to create custom workflows and automate tasks.

Remember, exploring advanced features and tools may require some time and practice. Don't be afraid to experiment and learn at your own pace. The world of technology is ever-evolving, and there are always new features and tools to discover

Using Smartphones and Computers for Productivity Tasks

Using smartphones and computers for productivity tasks can significantly improve your efficiency and organization in both personal and professional settings. Here are some ways to leverage these devices for productivity:

1. Productivity Apps:

- Explore productivity apps that help you stay organized, manage tasks, and boost productivity. Some popular productivity apps include Todoist, Trello, Microsoft To Do, and Google Keep.

2. Email Management:

- Use your smartphone or computer's email client to manage your emails efficiently. Create folders, apply labels, and use filters to organize your inbox effectively.

3. Calendar and Scheduling:

- Sync your calendar across devices to stay on top of appointments, meetings, and events. Set reminders and use scheduling apps like Google Calendar or Microsoft Outlook for efficient time management.

4. Note-Taking and Document Collaboration:

- Utilize note-taking apps like Evernote, Microsoft OneNote, or Google Keep to jot down ideas, create to-do lists, and save important information that syncs across your devices.
- For collaborative work, use cloud-based document platforms like Google Workspace (formerly G Suite) or Microsoft 365 to collaborate with colleagues in real-time.

5. Task and Project Management:

- Employ project management tools like Asana, Basecamp, or Microsoft Planner to plan, track progress, and collaborate on projects efficiently.

6. Time Tracking and Pomodoro Technique:

- Use time-tracking apps to monitor how you spend your time and identify areas for improvement.
- Consider implementing the Pomodoro Technique, which involves working in focused intervals (e.g., 25 minutes) followed by short breaks to boost productivity.

7. Scanning and Digital Document Management:

- Utilize your smartphone's camera or dedicated scanning apps to digitize physical documents, receipts, or notes. Save them as PDFs for easy access and organization.

8. Voice-to-Text Dictation:

- Leverage voice-to-text dictation features on your devices to compose emails, write documents, or take notes efficiently without typing.

9. Password Managers:

- Improve security and save time by using password managers to securely store and auto-fill your login credentials across websites and apps.

10. Keyboard Shortcuts:

- Learn keyboard shortcuts for commonly used actions, such as copy, paste, undo, and switching between open applications, to speed up your workflow.

11. Digital File Organization:

- Create well-organized folders and directories on your computer and cloud storage to keep files easily accessible and avoid clutter.

By effectively using smartphones and computers for productivity tasks, you can streamline your workflow, increase efficiency, and accomplish more in your daily life. Remember to find the tools and apps that best suit your needs and preferences. Regularly explore new productivity apps and features to stay updated with the latest advancements in technology.

Entertainment Options: Streaming Media and Gaming

Entertainment options on smartphones and computers have expanded dramatically in recent years, providing an array of streaming media and gaming experiences. Here are some exciting ways to enjoy entertainment on your devices:

Streaming Media:

1. **Video Streaming Services:**
   - Subscribe to popular video streaming services like Netflix, Amazon Prime Video, Hulu, Disney+, or Apple TV+ to access a vast library of movies, TV shows, and original content.

2. **Live TV Streaming:**
   - Explore live TV streaming services such as YouTube TV, Sling TV, or Hulu + Live TV to watch live sports, news, and TV channels without a traditional cable subscription.

3. **Music Streaming Services:**
   - Use music streaming platforms like Spotify, Apple Music, Amazon Music, or Tidal to access millions of songs, create personalized playlists, and discover new music.

4. **Podcasts and Audiobooks:**
    - Listen to podcasts on various topics and genres using podcast apps like Apple Podcasts, Spotify, or Google Podcasts.
    - Enjoy audiobooks through platforms like Audible or Librivox for immersive literary experiences.

Gaming:

1. **Mobile Gaming:**
    - Explore a vast selection of mobile games available on app stores (iOS and Android). From casual games to complex adventures, there's something for every gaming preference.
2. **PC and Console Gaming:**
    - For a more immersive gaming experience, play PC games or console games on gaming consoles like PlayStation, Xbox, or Nintendo Switch.
3. **Cloud Gaming:**
    - Try cloud gaming services like Google Stadia, NVIDIA GeForce Now, or Xbox Cloud Gaming (formerly Project xCloud) to stream games directly

to your device without the need for powerful hardware.

4. **Online Multiplayer Gaming:**
    - Engage in online multiplayer games with friends and gamers worldwide. Join cooperative missions, competitive battles, or massive open-world experiences.

Virtual Reality (VR) and Augmented Reality (AR):

1. **VR Gaming and Experiences:**
    - Immerse yourself in VR gaming with headsets like Oculus Rift, HTC Vive, or PlayStation VR, offering unique gaming experiences and simulations.
2. **AR Apps and Games:**
    - Explore augmented reality apps and games that blend virtual elements with the real world, allowing you to interact with digital objects in your environment.

Online Streaming and Gaming Communities:

1. **Social Streaming Platforms:**
    - Join live streaming communities like Twitch, YouTube Gaming, or Facebook Gaming to watch live gameplay and interact with streamers and fellow viewers.
2. **Gaming Forums and Communities:**
    - Participate in gaming forums, subreddits, or online communities related to your favorite games, platforms, or genres to discuss strategies, share tips, and connect with other gamers.

With the abundance of streaming media and gaming options available, you can tailor your entertainment experience to suit your preferences and interests. From binge-watching your favorite TV shows to embarking on epic gaming adventures, smartphones and computers offer endless entertainment possibilities.

CONCLUSION

Congratulations on completing the journey of "Tech Demystified: A Layman's Guide to Navigating Smartphones and Computers." Throughout this book, we embarked on an enlightening exploration of the ever-evolving world of technology, aiming to empower you with the knowledge and confidence to make the most of your smartphones and computers.

From the basics of understanding your devices to venturing into advanced features and tools, we've covered a wide range of topics to cater to both beginners and seasoned users. Our mission was to demystify the intricacies of technology, making it accessible and enjoyable for everyone.

In the initial chapters, we laid the foundation by introducing you to the fundamentals of smartphones and computers. We discussed hardware components, operating systems, and the essential functions that form the backbone of these devices. Understanding the terminology and functionalities provided a strong starting point for our journey.

As we progressed, we delved into the realm of applications and digital experiences. From productivity tools that enhance efficiency to entertainment options like streaming media and gaming, we explored the endless possibilities that smartphones and computers offer in enriching our lives.

Throughout the book, our focus remained on simplicity and clarity. We broke down complex concepts into digestible pieces, ensuring that you gained a comprehensive understanding without feeling overwhelmed. Our goal was to provide you with a practical guide that you can refer to as you navigate your digital journey.

We also emphasized the importance of staying safe and secure in the digital landscape. Understanding internet safety, privacy measures, and how to protect your personal information became paramount in our discussions. Empowering you with knowledge to avoid common pitfalls and protect yourself from online threats was of utmost importance.

Remember that technology is a dynamic field, constantly evolving and introducing new possibilities. As you continue your journey beyond this book, embrace curiosity and the willingness to explore further. Embrace the continuous advancements in technology with an open mind, knowing that you have the foundation to adapt and thrive.

Our sincere hope is that "Tech Demystified" has ignited your passion for technology, allowing you to embrace these devices as tools of empowerment rather than sources of confusion. Embrace the digital world with confidence, and let technology be a conduit for creativity, productivity, and meaningful connections.

As we conclude this journey, remember that technology is not merely a collection of circuits and code; it is a gateway to knowledge, communication, and endless possibilities. Let your curiosity drive you to explore, learn, and harness the potential that technology holds.

Thank you for joining us in this exploration of smartphones and computers. We hope that the knowledge you've gained will empower you to make the most of these incredible devices. As technology continues to shape our world, let your journey be filled with discovery, growth, and exciting new experiences.

Safe travels on your digital path, and may you continue to thrive in the ever-evolving landscape of technology.

Happy navigating!

© Copyright 2023 by Nathan R. Jankins - All rights reserved.

Printed in Great Britain
by Amazon